Capture Greater
Lehigh Valley

The Best of the Lehigh Valley in Photography

Presented by

Foreword

Historical architecture. Untouched wild lands. Sports. The stunning changing of Northern seasons. Favorite foods. The arts. Our hobbies. Our homes. This collection not only *Captures* the Greater Lehigh Valley — it also vibrantly, joyfully and thoughtfully *Celebrates* it.

The call to action for photographs for Capture Greater Lehigh Valley was not taken lightly; as evidenced by more than 15,000 entries submitted by 356 talented photographers and finally, nearly 1.5 million views and 500,000 votes from community members. It's a reminder that the spirit of the Greater Lehigh Valley cannot be defined simply.

A vast merger of cultures, traditions, ideas and innovations through the centuries has created a presence that is both ever-changing and ever-grounded. And what better testimony than photographs to portray glimpses of daily life in the Greater Lehigh Valley as well as events we've witnessed in business, political and educational landscapes? Our deep history and our hopeful future are narrated beautifully through each image.

In addition to familiar scenes, you will find new treasures and great pride on the pages ahead. Enjoy each moment that Captures and Celebrates the Greater Lehigh Valley.

PBS 39

–Your PBS39 Team

Table of Contents

About This Book

Capture Greater Lehigh Valley™ is a unique approach to fine-art book publishing. An online community of local photographers submitted photos to be considered for this book. Then, area residents voted to determine which photos would be published. From 15,297 photo submissions to the pages of this book, 444,770 votes helped shape what you hold in your hands. It's the Greater Lehigh Valley through the eyes and lenses of local photographers and enthusiasts. Enjoy!

Join the Community

Every bit of this book was made possible by an active community of users on the Capture Greater Lehigh Valley Web site. Whether you're a professional photographer, hobbyist, or just like looking at great Lehigh Valley photography, join the community at Capture Greater Lehigh Valley (capturelehighvalley.com).

How to Use This Book

Open. Look at the best photography you've ever seen. Repeat. Actually, maybe there's a little more to it. First, be sure to note the credit listed with each photo. Search for your favorite photographer at Capture Greater Lehigh Valley (capturelehighvalley.com) and leave your comment or show your appreciation with a vote. Many photographers also sell their photos online so you may be able to buy a print for your wall! Also note, captions are used as submitted by the photographer, mostly verbatim. We do our best to fact check, but captions may not be perfect.

Copyright Details

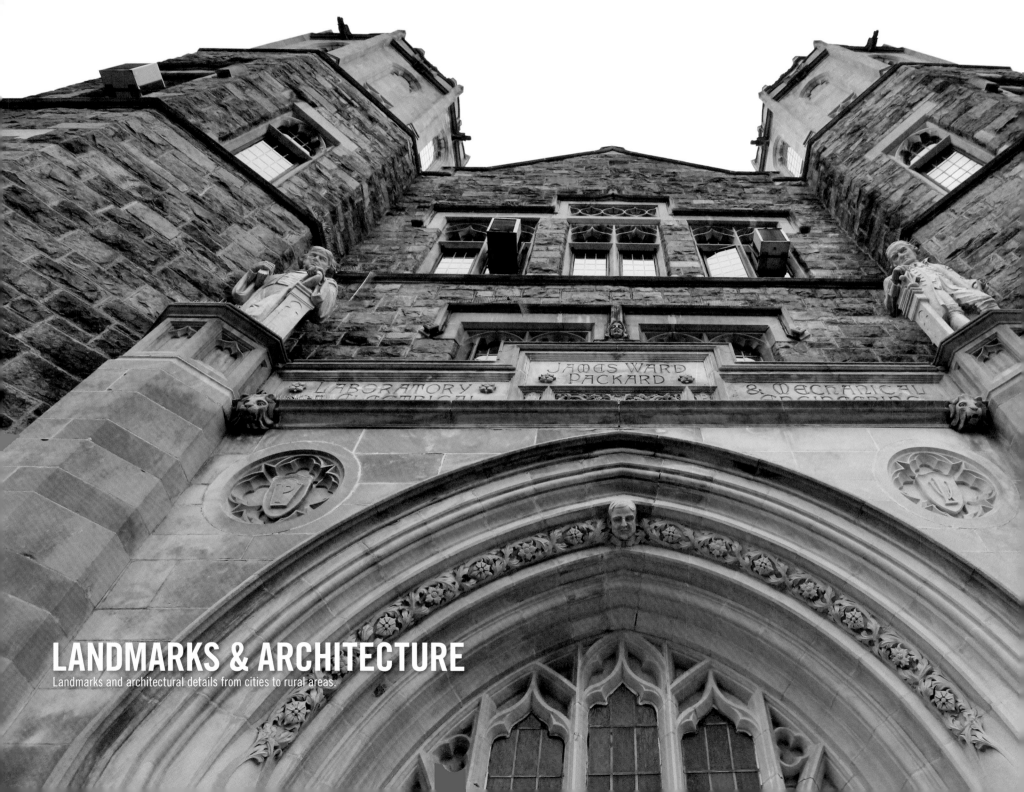

LANDMARKS & ARCHITECTURE
Landmarks and architectural details from cities to rural areas.

THE GUIDING LIGHT BY RUTH DENNISON (above): Bethlehem by night.

EVERYONES WELCOME BY MAYOLA MANN (left): One of the many beautiful churches in Catasauqua.

PACKARD LAB BY TIM HOLMES (far left): Lehigh University building.

OLD CHURCH BELL TOWER BY DENISE MOSER (above): In black and white.

LOVELY LOWHILL BY M HESS (top): Founded in 1769, Lowhill Church (now known as Christ's Church at Lowhill UCC) is an important historic landmark in New Tripoli Township, at Lowhill's north end.

LINDERMAN LIBRARY BY TIM HOLMES (right): Library entrance on the campus of Lehigh University.

HUFF'S UNION CHURCH BY TOM SCHERER (far right): A clear blue sky and the golden tones of autumn make up the backdrop for this view of Huff's Union Church.

JACOB NICHOLAS HOUSE BY OMAR MORALES (above): Jacob Nicholas house.

PARKING LINES BY JONATHAN DAVIES (left): Parking garage on 8th Street in Allentown.

STEEL COMPANY OFFICES BY JIM WILLIAMS (opposite): Old offices from the plant side.

ICE CREAM ON BANK STREET BY ELIZABETH WYANT (above): Ice cream at the Purple Cow Creamery on Bank St. in Easton.

TRIPLE FLOORS OF COLORED WINDOWS BY JEFF CUSHNER (1): Anyone who crosses the Tilghman Street Bridge over the Lehigh River knows this building, but we usually aren't looking to the sides when we're crossing.

BLAIRSTOWN DINER BY KERRY SNYDER (2): This diner was one of our stops on a little "Friday the 13th" scene tour. Aside from being used in the movie, this iconic diner and its awesome chrome, red and glass block look, is a great stop if you are ever in Blairstown. Great hometown feel and great home town diner food!

OLD ALLENTOWN MEETS THE NEW BY JEFFRY GRIM (3): Pennsylvania Power and Light building reflected in the Butz building, 9th & Hamilton Streets.

BEAUTIFUL VIEW BY MAYOLA MANN (4): Looking out what is the store to the actual furnace at Hopewell Furnace.

6TH & NORTHAMPTON BY JEFF DAYHOFF (5): Apartment building on 500 block of Northampton Street.

PPL BUILDING - ALLENTOWN, PA BY THOMAS GRIM (6): PPL (formerly Pennsylvania Power & Light Company) building in downtown Allentown. This building was built in 1926-1927.

BLUE SHUTTERS BY KEN SOUSER (7): Old schoolhouse.

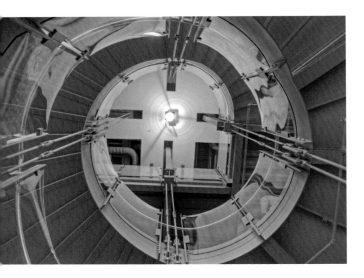

ARTSSTEPS BY JEFFRY GRIM (above): ArtsQuest Center, Bethlehem.

PAGODA AT NIGHT BY JESSICA PETROHOY (right): Reading Pagoda Skyline.

LEHIGH UNIVERSITY CAMPUS BY JOHN DELGROSSO (far right): Lehigh University campus.

LEATHER CORNER POST HOTEL BY ROBERT SANDER (below): Vintage hotel in Leather Corner Post.

UNDER THE BRIDGE BY CHRIS LACOUR (above): A long exposure brings out the colors from under the Northampton Street Bridge.

COVERED BRIDGE FLOOR BY JEFF CUSHNER (left): Guth's covered bridge.

REFLECTION BY RICHARD SIPOS (opposite): Water and bridge underpass taken at Lockridge Furnace, Alburtis.

THE MAIN HOUSE BY BENITO CRUZ JR (above): I love this building and going out to Glasbern.

EIGHTH STREET BRIDGE HDR BY LEROY KROMIS (opposite top left): Underneath the 8th Street Bridge in Allentown. Taken at sunset, for light to strike the underside of the bridge.

AN EARLY SNOW BY CAROLYN LANDI (opposite top right): A non traditional view of Kreidersville covered bridge while still snowing. The tire tracks from my car added interest, I thought.

MORAVIAN DOORS BY JOHN DELGROSSO (opposite bottom): Moravian Doors.

PORTALS AT LOCKRIDGE FURNACE BY ROBERT SANDER (opposite right): Artistic interpretation of rail track supports at Lockridge Furnace.

OLD WAGON WHEELS BY JEAN KRANTZ (above left): Barn on the Troxell-Steckel farmhouse property.

SMALL LOG CABIN, LEHIGH PARKWAY, ALLENTOWN, PA BY THOMAS GRIM (above right): Log cabin.

ROAD SIDE BARN BY SANTAMARIA WAGNER (right): Road side barn.

HONEY HOLE BY DJ FLOREK (left): Located near Springtown and Saucon Valley. I think the television show, "American Pickers," would like this place.

CEMENT CITY BY ETHAN QUIN (below): The Coplay Cement Kilns off the Ironton Rail-Trail.

FUN: GREATER LEHIGH VALLEY STYLE

Sports, recreation, celebration, festivals, food and music in the Greater Lehigh Valley.

OH NOOOO! BY RICHARD HAFNER (above): Runner will be out.

BALLS & GLOVE BY LISA SEIFERT (left): Bucket o'balls.

BEST SEATS IN THE HOUSE BY TIM HOLMES (far left): Right around the corner.

COCA-COLA PARK BY ETHAN QUIN (above): Another day at the ball game.

PIGS AND HENS BY JOE ROB (right): Toledo Mudhens vs. Lehigh Valley Iron Pigs.

PLAYMAKER BY LORI YOUNG (above left): On the move.

LOOK I'M WINNING BY TODD FRITZ (above right): These little guys are so funny to watch.

WHEN IT IS STILL JUST A GAME BY TIM HOLMES (left): Freshman football.

EARLY FISHING BY CAROL TERSINE (following left): Fishing in the mist.

SILHOUETTES OF BOYS FISHING AT SUNSET
BY A. GURMANKIN (following right top): Boys fishing at sunset.

RED CANOES BY CAROLYN LANDI (following bottom left): Every year we go canoeing. We always have a great time.

FISHING AT MINSI LAKE
BY GEORGINA WRIGHT LONG (following bottom right): Big mouth bass.

HIKING THE FALLS BY ANNE DALE (above): Hiking the falls.

FISHING BY JESSICA PETROHOY (right top): It was the golden hour and I managed to capture this quiet scene of what looks like a father and son fishing.

ON TOP OF THE WORLD BY BETHANN PASQUALE (right bottom): The Pinnacle, Hamburg.

CLIMBING TRIUMVIRATE DIRECT, MT. TAMANY, DELAWARE WATER GAP BY CHRIS LACOUR (far right): A climber grips the small edges of the popular climbing route, Triumvirate Direct, high above Interstate 80 on the cliffs of Mt. Tammany.

READY TO ROLL BY GENE FERNANDEZ (above): Pocono Raceway.

IN FRONT BY LEROY BOGERT (left): Quarter Midget Racing.

BIG AIR TRICK BY LEROY BOGERT (opposite left top): Big air contest.

POWER OFF THE CORNER BY LEROY BOGERT (opposite left bottom): Catch me if you can.

BETHLEHEM SKATEPLAZA BY LORI YOUNG (opposite right): You turn me upside down.

STROLLING DOWN MAIN STREET BY JOHN CASTELINE (left): Bethlehem Half Marathon, October 2012.

RUNNERS BY JANE GEIST (bottom left): Mom and daughter participate in the 2013 St. Patrick's Day 5K.

THE GIRL AND THE WHITE HORSE BY PETER NEWMAN (bottom right): The girl on the white horse at the rodeo in Nazareth.

IRON HILL TWILIGHT CLASSIC BY JAMIE MARRERO (opposite): Bike racing under the streetlights.

COLOR IN DISARRAY BY JONATHAN DAVIES (above): Laser tag at Lehigh Valley Laser Tag.
MY BLUE AVATAR TREE II BY MAYOLA MANN (right): A different perspective of the tree.

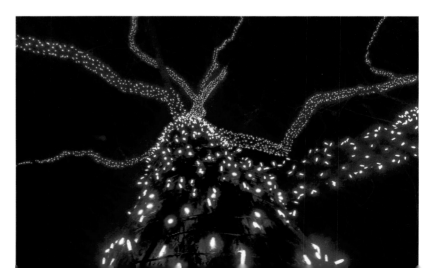

CRIMSON CHRISTMAS BY DEAN HAWKEY (left): Christkindlmarkt.

MAKING CHRISTMAS ORNAMENTS BY RICHARD SIPOS (far left): Christkindlmarkt ornament maker.

STEEL STACKS CARRIAGE RIDE BY RICHARD SIPOS (below): Christkindlmarkt Steel Stacks carriage ride.

CONFETTI CAFE BY DJ FLOREK (following left): The Christmas spirit is alive on Main Street.

HOLIDAY HORSE BY JONATHAN DAVIES (following right): Girl meets horse at Christkindlmarkt.

BALLOON RIDE BY LINDA ZAK (above): Above it all.

HOODS BY TOM SCHERER (left top): Car hoods at the Wheels of Time Rod & Custom car show.

UP AND AWAY BY PHILIP KRESGE (left bottom): I had always wanted to take a ride in a hot air balloon. My wife, Betsy, gave me the opportunity with her Christmas gift to me. As the balloon began to ascend, I looked up and saw this wonderful sight that, to me, summed up the whole experience.

STEARMAN LOVE BY STACIE MCKEEVER (opposite): Wax day for the Biplane.

WANT TO GO UP BY JEAN KRANTZ (above): Nice place to be at dusk. Cool sky, warm lights.

STEEL FORCE RIDERS AT SUNSET BY LEROY KROMIS (left top): Taken at the beginning of last season and has been on my photostream. All I can say is that I love cloudy sunsets.

THE GREAT ALLENTOWN FAIR LIT UP THE NIGHT BY CHRISTINE ISAKOFF (left bottom): Night time Ferris wheel view.

UNTITLED BY VINNIE ZOUTENBIER (right): July Fourth at the Steel Stacks with the community.

THE LOOK OF LOVE BY HOANG NGUYEN (above): There is no better photo than those of the two being in love.

INDIAN POW-WOW BY CHUCK HIXSON (opposite top left): Performer at Pow-Wow at Lenape Museum in Allentown.

EMISH AT CELTIC CLASSIC BY LEROY KROMIS (opposite top right): Christy Brown the group's fiddler. She is part of a great Celtic band based in Port Jervis, New York.

MAKING CANDLES BY GEORGINA WRIGHT LONG (opposite bottom left): Animal fat candle making at Quiet Valley Historical Farm's Fall Festival.

RE-ENACTING A SKIRMISH BY JEFFRY GRIM (opposite bottom middle): Camp Geiger, Whitehall PA.

CELTIC FEST BY LORI YOUNG (opposite bottom right): An amazing show of strength.

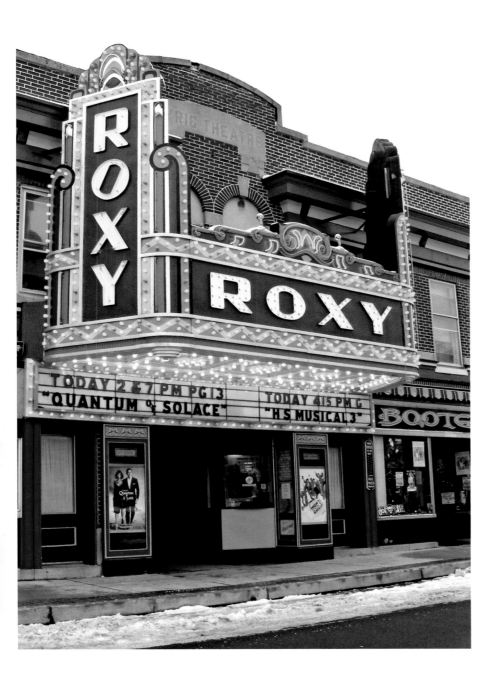

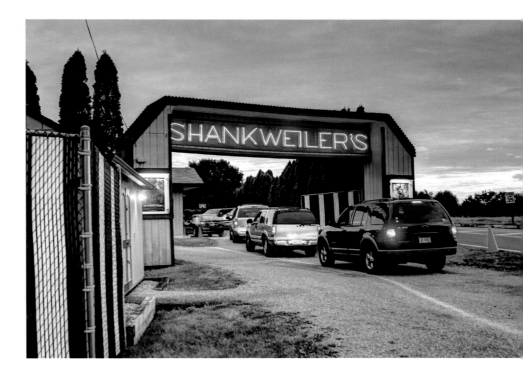

SHANKWEILERS DRIVE-IN BY LEROY BOGERT (above): Shankweilers Drive-in is the oldest drive-in in the U.S. and continues to this day to be a part of my family.

LET US ENTERTAIN YOU BY CAROLYN LANDI (left): Many great bands have played here and a million movies...a great place to visit and be entertained. Love the architecture of the building and the nostalgia of the era.

SHANE COOLEY BY ETHAN QUIN (opposite left): Shane Cooley and his father perform at Hart Fest 2010 in Walnutport, PA.

NICK HEXUM - 311 BY MATT CHRISTINE (opposite right): 311, performing on July 31st at the Sands Event Center in Bethlehem, PA.

GOO GOO DOLLS BY LORI YOUNG (above): Goo Goo Dolls put on quite a show at Musikfest.

LZZY HALE - HALESTORM BY MATT CHRISTINE (1): Halestorm, performing on June 30th at the Sherman Theater in Stroudsburg, PA.

JUST PLAYIN' DA BLUES BY ROBERT BECKER (2): Blues guitarist at the Blues Festival at Steel Stacks.

JESSE COOK CONCERT SERIES III BY MAYOLA MANN (3): Jesse Cook and Nicolas Hernandez.

PLAYING A LITTLE STREET MUSIC BY RAY SLAVINSKI (4): Just playing around by the old hotel.

OFTEN IMITATED, NEVER DUPLICATED BY JAMIE MARRERO (5): The Liberty High School Grenadier Band.

FARM FRESH FOOD
BY ELIZABETH WYANT (top): Farm fresh food at the Easton Farmers' Market.

SCARECROW FESTIVAL
BY ELIZABETH WYANT (far left): View of Scarecrow Festival, Easton Farmers' Market, Easton.

HARVEST TIME
BY JIM DAVIS (bottom left): Reaping the benefits of a good summer.

HEART BERRIES
BY DJ FLOREK (bottom right): Two heart shaped strawberries.

PURITY BY PHILIP KRESGE (left): In glass blowing, the purity is the steel rod that is used to transfer the piece from the blowpipe. Additional shaping can then be completed, including widening the opening of the vessel. Taken at Glass Works, Banana Factory, Bethlehem.

LONGWOOD GARDENS BY SUSAN BROWN (below): A photo club was there the day we were. They were given waders and allowed in the lily ponds.

ARTIST IN THE ROSE GARDEN BY THOMAS GRIM (above): Artists from the Bethlehem Palette Club enjoy the day painting scenes at the beautiful Allentown Rose Garden.

PUMPKINS AT RENNINGERS FARM MARKET - KUTZTOWN, PA BY DONALD CAMPOLONGO (opposite left top): Pumpkins.

SWEET FOREVER BY JESSICA LEE (opposite left bottom): Delectable sweets for the sweet.

HIBACHI STYLE BY CAROLYN LANDI (opposite right): Hibachi chef at Desaki cooking up some good eats.

PEOPLE

Family, friends, children and other portraits of characters across the Greater Lehigh Valley.

RAGGEDY BY STACIE MCKEEVER (above): Worn raggedy by Charly.

GOTTA LOVE FOOTBALL!! BY DENISE MOSER (left): This is where it all begins!

MADDY AND PUMPKINS BY KATIE BALLANTINE (far left): Beautiful Maddy sitting in pumpkins.

DESTINATION UNKNOWN BY BETHANN PASQUALE (above): Train ride at Jim Thorpe.

POWER OUTAGE BY HOANG NGUYEN (1): Just when I thought they were deep in their sleep!!

HIKING BREAK BY DAVID PASQUALE (2): The Pinnacle, Hamburg.

COUSINS BY LORI WARSING (3): Enjoying a warm day at the park in December.

HAVING FUN!! BY JAMES LOBUE (4): Having Fun!!

SASSY LOOK BY KATIE BALLANTINE (5): My daughter at Weaver's Orchard getting a pumpkin.

LAZY MORNING 2 BY HOANG NGUYEN (above left): Family life.

BETHLEHEM, PENNSYLVANIA BY JEFFREY BELL (above right): Bethlehem, PA.

HAPPINESS BY OMAR MORALES (left): Mother and son enjoying a day at the park.

LAUGHIN' LADIES BY JOE MCCRACKEN (opposite): Laughin' ladies.

RIVERSIDE BY DONALD CARAVELLO (above): Family stopped along the river to skip some rocks.

FAMILY BY BRANDEE KRYCIA (right): Jake, Cole and Lauren taking a walk in beauty of downtown Bethlehem.

NEW YEARS EVE WEDDING BY KATIE BALLANTINE (left): This couple was married in the bride's childhood home on New Years Eve. What a special wedding!

JAY & ASHLEY BY TABITHA LASSO (bottom left): Engagement photo taken at the Musikfest area.

THE LOOK OF LOVE BY HOANG NGUYEN (bottom right): A National Guard soldier spending quality time with his fiancee.

MANS BEST FRIEND BY JONATHAN DAVIES (above): A man and iguana on a stroll at Celtic Fest.

DAPPER DAN BY RICHARD HAFNER (left): New photo for his promo cards. Dan wanted a headshot for cards he hands out.

UNTITLED BY PAUL SELL (below): Natural light portrait made in a vacant warehouse.

A BAD DAY OF FISHING IS BETTER THAN A... BY TIM HOLMES (opposite): Great fishing spot!

FURRY FRIENDS
Pets, farm animals and creatures from the zoos.

COWS BY KEN SOUSER (above): Dinner rush hour in the country.

BEST IN SNOW BY DEAN WILEY (left): Our rescue, Shelby, having a blast in the snow.

MY KITTAH BY TIM HOLMES (far left): Kittah, at about 4 months old.

KOI SHOW BY JEAN KRANTZ (above): They used to have a Koi Competition at AgHall, but I haven't seen it scheduled there for years.

BEBE BY RICHARD HAFNER (left): BeBe is the 2013 mascot for Northampton County Special Olympics.

WHICH WAY DO I GO? BY CAROLYN LANDI (1): My sweet little kitty, Shredder, playing in a tree in my yard.

IT'S CHRISTMAS!! BY LORI LEWIS (2): Toby patiently waiting for Santa.

IT WON'T GET AWAY ON MY WATCH BY DEAN WILEY (3): Lennox hiding behind the slider shade planning his attack on the ball in the foreground.

QUEEN OF THE COUCH BY JANARA HOPPOCK (4): This is my adopted next door neighbor's cat, which we believe is a Birman cat.

OUR COCKATIEL... BY DENISE MOSER (5): Yes, he does have an attitude and knows how to use it!

WAITING FOR A PUSH... BY DENISE MOSER (6): She was loving the swing ride and didn't want to get out.

THIS LITTLE PIGGY... BY AMBER N (right): A mother pig and her piglets had all the attention at the Kutztown Fair.

PRIVACY PLE-E-E-ASE!! BY JAMES LOBUE (below): Privacy Ple-e-e-ase!!

**DON'T COUNT YOUR CHICKENS BEFORE THEY HATCH
BY DEBRA MICHALOWSKI** (left): Which eggs are mine?
Taken at Apple Ridge Farm.

TURKEY POSSE BY M HESS (bottom left): Out for a
forage, or perhaps to test crossing the road along
Route 143.

**UP CLOSE AND PERSONAL
BY RICHARD GROULEFF** (bottom right): Appaloosa
close up.

SCAPES OF ALL SORTS

Landscapes, waterscapes and other dramatic scenes of the Greater Lehigh Valley.

WINTER RAINBOW BY M HESS (above): Heavy cloud cover and mist after a winter storm transform the morning commute at Cedar Crest Boulevard and Walbert Avenue.

CONTRAST IN WHITE AND RED BY JEFF CUSHNER (left): On the way to fall kayaking at Lake Nockamixon.

LONE TREE ON HAWK MOUNTAIN ROAD BY MICHAEL PYLE (far left): Lone tree on Hawk Mountain Road.

GOLDEN PASSAGE BY KEN SOUSER (above): Conrad Lane near Landis Store.

EVERYONE HAS TO TAKE AT LEAST ONE... BY DENISE MOSER (right): Picture of beautiful fall colored trees reflecting in the water.

THE LANE BY CAROL COMMINS (opposite): Taken in Upper Mt. Bethel.

SNOWGEESE BY RUTH DENNISON (right): Snowgeese in flight path over the Hunsicker Farm.

EARLY BY CAROL TERSINE (far right): Fog in fall.

BEACON BY ETHAN QUIN (below): The most familiar can be the most alien.

THREE WINTER TREES BY STACIE MCKEEVER (opposite): Waiting for the thaw.

PULPIT ROCK SUNRISE BY MICHAEL PYLE (above): Pulpit Rock sunrise.

SUNSET BY CHRISTINE ISAKOFF (1): Beautiful September sunset.

THE BEAUTY OF WINTER BY RICHARD GROULEFF (2): Colorful late winter sunset captured at the Indian Tower.

WINTER SUNSET FENCE AT RODALE PARK HDR BY LEROY KROMIS (3): Shot along the north side fence at Rodale Park in Trexlertown.

AS A NEW DAY DAWNS BY DENISE MOSER (4): The evening fades away.

DORNEY PARK'S STEEL FORCE AT SUNSET BY LEROY KROMIS (5): A winter sunset with Steel Force reflected in the water.

GOLDEN FIELDS BY CHRIS DEMCHAK (6): Seen where rural and urban unite.

GLEN ONOKO FALLS BY DANIELLE DAVIDHEISER (above): One of my favorite places to hike. :)

AFTER THE RAIN BY CAROL TERSINE (left): Nature at its best.

DAWN ON THE RIVER BY ROBERT BECKER (far left): Breaking dawn on the Delaware River near Bushkill.

BRIDESMAID FALLS AT BUSHKILL BY MICHAEL PYLE (above): The Bridesmaid Falls at Bushkill, PA.

LOST BOAT BY OMAR MORALES (right): Abandoned boat at the Lehigh River Dam in Palmer.

HILL CHURCH BY KEN SOUSER (above): Fall beauty.

THE CHAPEL BY MICHAEL PYLE (opposite left top): The chapel at Hickory Run.

THE OLD STONE SPRING HOUSE BY CAROLYN BARNES (opposite left middle): This used to be the water cooler.

CLOVER KNOLL FARM BY SUSAN BROWN (opposite left bottom): A beautifully kept farm.

BARN REFLECTION BY LEROY BOGERT (opposite right): I have gone past this for years, and never stopped to photograph this. What was I thinking?

GRIST MILL BY ROBERT BECKER (above): A historic Grist Mill sits on Scenic Drive near a stream in Point Philip, PA.

JIM THORPE BY DEAN WILEY (right): Jim Thorpe as seen from the top of Flagstaff Mountain.

THE SKYLINE BY JONATHAN DAVIES (following left): An Allentown Sky.

CITYSCAPING BY MAYOLA MANN (following right): I never would have thought I would like photographing cityscapes in large cities, but I have found another avenue of photography that I am enjoying immensely! This is inferred processed, hope you like it as much as I do. :)

ROAD TO HAWK MOUNTAIN BY M HESS (above): A bleak but lovely landscape dusted with an early snowfall, Hawk Mountain possesses compelling beauty in any season.

FOGGY MORNING WALK EAST BY KERRY SNYDER (right): It was a very foggy morning on the New Jersey side of the Roebling's Riegelsville Bridge (opened in 1904). Even though it only spans 577 feet, you couldn't even see the other side!

ABANDONED LOT BY CHRIS LACOUR (left): Snow covers the weeds that grow through the pavement of an abandoned lot in Easton.

PHILLIPSBURG, NJ TINY TOWN BY JEFF CUSHNER (bottom left): Flickr Explore 12/21/08 #292.

HOMES NEAR FLOOD STAGE ON LEHIGH RIVER BY THOMAS GRIM (bottom right): Homes on Adams Island.

FREIGHT HOUSE
GIFT SHOP

TO TRAINS↑

TICKETS

LOCOMOTIVE
CAB RIDES

ASK TICKET AGENT
FOR DETAILS

OFF TO SCHOOL BY JUAN GARCIA (above): Alex Garcia getting on the bus and off to school.

A TRAIN RIDE BY JOE ROB (left): An idle train in Jim Thorpe.

NEW HOPE IVYLAND TRAIN STATION BY JAN GOLTZ (far left): Decked out for the holiday.

BETHLEHEM STEEL BY JESSICA PETROHOY (right): A symbol of Bethlehem, PA and its industrial history.

OLD GEARS BY ELIZABETH WYANT (bottom left): Old gears on Canal. Hugh Moore Park, Easton PA.

SIDE TRACKED BY STACIE MCKEEVER (bottom right): Sitting silent.

SHELL BY JAMIE MARRERO (opposite): The shell of one of the many Bethlehem Steel Buildings waiting for its time to be brought back to life.

WHAT LIES WITHIN BY ETHAN WALLACE (above): Partially disassembled gas-blowing engine, Bethlehem Steel.

SOUNDS OF STEEL BY RUTH DENNISON (right): Bethlehem Steel Museum.

THE LONG WALK BY TOM SCHERER (far right): Walkway to the control tower in Norfolk-Southern's Allentown Yard.

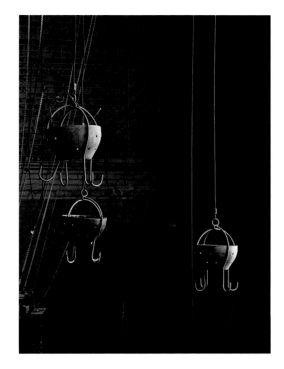

STEEL INTRIGUE BY DEAN HAWKEY (above): Know what these are? They are found in the old locker rooms at the Bethlehem Steel. They were once used to hoist valuables to the ceiling and then locked while showering.

ARCH SUPPORT BY GENE FERNANDEZ (left): Steel Stacks tribute flame, Bethlehem.

NMIH NIGHT PHOTO SHOOT BY FRANK SATTLER (above): Wheel in the sky.

BUSY NITE BY FRANK SATTLER (left): Busy nite of steel pouring.

STEEL SKY BY BRANDEE KRYCIA (far left): The Bethlehem Steel Stacks light up on a beautiful clear night.

APIARIST (BEEKEEPER) BY RICHARD HAFNER (above): Every spring supers must be added before the honey flow begins. Just happens to also be my dad!

HOMESTEAD GARDEN BY DJ FLOREK (right): Step through the arbor to a wonderful homestead garden.

LOOKING UP BY JESSICA PETROHOY (opposite): Windmill Farms, Landis Store, PA.

BARN 4 BY KEN SOUSER (below): Warmth of the late afternoon sun.

CORN CRIB SUNRISE BY STACIE MCKEEVER (above): Early morning on the field.

MAIL POUCH TOBACCO BY JOSEPH KLOSS (right): An early form of billboard advertising and an extra source of income to farmers of the day.

FARM IN THE FALL BY TOM SCHERER (far right): Captured in the late afternoon light of autumn.

HARVESTING CORN BY DONALD CAMPOLONGO (above): Corn harvest with a Case Combine.

4TH OF JULY BY JAMIE MARRERO (left): An early harvest on the 4th of July.

TEAM WORK BY GENE FERNANDEZ (far left): Farming the way it was.

HARVEST BY STACIE MCKEEVER (above): Break time for John Deere.

FALL CARROTS BY PIE BIRD (1): Early fall carrots, bunched and ready to go to our farm members.

PUMPKIN PATCH BY LEROY BOGERT (2): Ready for the picking.

FALL FANTASTIC BY KERRY SNYDER (3): All the wonderful colors of fall in one ear of corn from Traugers Farm Market.

POTATO PATCH BY RICHARD HAFNER (4): Plants are in bloom, however, pollination of the flowers is not required for the tubers to form.

PUMPKIN BY DJ FLOREK (5): Time to pick a pumpkin at Traugers Farm Market.

GRAPES FOR THE WINE BY CAROL COMMINS (6): Taken at Franklin Hill Vineyards.

ABANDONED BY JESSICA PETROHOY (above left): Overgrown fire hydrant at an abandoned industrial park.

DECISIONS BY LOU WHEELAND (above right): Western Salisbury fire chief Josh Wells on scene.

HOT SILHOUETTE BY LOU WHEELAND (right): Cetronia firefighter.

ON THE AIR BY GENE FERNANDEZ (opposite): Master control at PBS39.

MICHELLE SPEAKS BY CAROLYN LANDI (top): Michelle Obama came to Moravian College to rally votes for her husband during the 2012 presidential campaign.

SELLING CHRISTMAS BY JONATHAN DAVIES (bottom): Preparing the crowd for the live advent calendar in Bethlehem.

BLACKSMITH AT WORK BY MARLENA KRCELICH (opposite left top): Blacksmith hard at work in downtown, historic Bethlehem.

MACK TRUCKS CUSTOMIZING TRUCK LINE BY THOMAS GRIM (opposite left bottom): Mack Trucks Museum.

FIXING THE ROOF BY GEORGINA WRIGHT LONG (opposite right): St. John's Windish Evangelical Lutheran Church gets some maintenance.

SCHOOL OF ART BY TONY CIMEROL (following left): Statue in front of The Baum School of Art in Allentown.

BETHLEHEM, PENNSYLVANIA BY JEFFREY BELL (following right top): Bethlehem, Penn.

KODACHROME WEEKLY BY DJ FLOREK (following bottom left): A Kodak 35RF camera on a copy of the Weekly Kodachrome publication. Captured during WWII Day.

REMEMBERING OUR SANDY HOOK CHILDREN BY CAROL TERSINE (following bottom right): Pray to keep children safe from all harm.

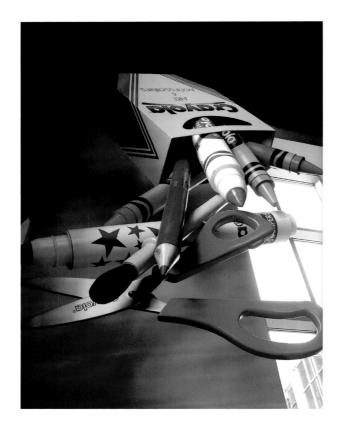

CRAYOLA FACTORY BY JACQUELINE LEWIS (above): Centerpiece for tourism in Easton and major manufacturer of fun stuff for kids of all ages.

SAUCON VALLEY CROSS COUNTRY BY RICHARD HAFNER (top left): Girl's team.

MARTIN GUITAR, MARTIN GUITAR, MARTIN GUITAR, ET AL
BY JEFFRY GRIM (top right): Making Martins at Martin Guitar, Nazareth PA.

A WHAT? A TYPEWRITER. BY JULIE LUBINSKY (bottom): Taken from inside the original 1910 New Tripoli Bank. From the looks of the chair, someone sat for a long time typing out things on this now antique machine called a typewriter! Reminds me how much I love my iPad.

NICE KNOCKERS BY LORI YOUNG (opposite): Muhlenberg College.

NATURE

The beautiful wildlife, stunning nature and dramatic weather of the Greater Lehigh Valley.

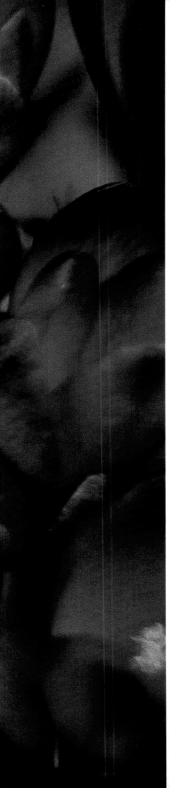

SPRING PREVIEW BY TOM SCHERER (above): Before long, it will be time for the grape hyacinths to bloom at Lockridge Furnace Park.

ON TOP OF IT BY GENE FERNANDEZ (left): Beautiful Swallowtail in our garden.

WHITE CROCUS BY ROBERT BECKER (far left): White Crocus stands out from its siblings.

ODD MAN OUT BY SCOTT SWARTLEY (above): Basically it's one flower vs. them all.

SINGLE FLOWER BY ROBERT BECKER (1): Single flower displayed at Nazareth Garden Show.

SPRING INSIDE BY JESSICA LEE (2): Macro shot of flower from my yard.

THE JOY OF GARDENING BY TOM SCHERER (3): It's nice to be able to take a few steps out of the house and be able to photograph flowers in my garden.

DREAMY BY TODD FRITZ (4): Taken at the Allentown Rose Gardens.

SUNNY FLOWERS BY ELIZABETH WYANT (5): Sunny flowers at the Easton Farmers' Market, Easton.

BLUE COLUMBINE BY THOMAS GRIM (6): Blue Columbine flower.

GET OFF MY BACK! BY GENE FERNANDEZ (above): Ladybug acting as a chauffeur.

BULLSEYE! BY JAN GOLTZ (left top): In my front yard. :-)

GREEDY CHIPMUNK BY CHUCK HIXSON (left bottom): This little guy actually fit both of these peanuts into his mouth and then scampered off. Hope he shared!

JULIE BY KERRY SNYDER (above): The cutest little frog that happened by our pond. My kids named it Julie. It looked a little different than the other frogs. We knew right away that it was her, she always looked so happy!

SPIDER & HER YOUNG BY ETHAN QUIN (left top): Found on the east side of Allentown, carrying her new babies on her back.

PRAYING MANTIS BY LORETTA LESTER (bottom left): Praying mantis poses for the camera.

WET WEB BY KERRY SNYDER (bottom right): A spider web on the Riegelsville Bridge on a VERY foggy morning.

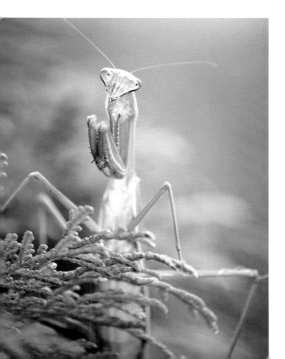

CARDINAL AND A PINE CONE
BY MICHAEL PYLE (right): Cardinal and a pine cone. Captured in Coopersburg, Penn.

EARLY FISHING
BY CAROL TERSINE (far right): Misty morning majesty.

BLUEBIRD WITH BERRY
BY PHILIP KRESGE (bottom left): Picked from the holly bush outside my office window.

OWL BY KEN SOUSER (bottom right): All in!

FAWN RESTING BY JOAN GILLEN (above left): We found this fawn resting on the side lawn of our property one early spring morning. Captured with my Nikon D5100.

BABY FOXES BY LAURIE MCCARTY (above right): These kit foxes were living in my sand mound!!!

IT'S COMING THIS WAY BY JEAN KRANTZ (right): Summer storm, June 3rd.

FOGGY SUNRISE BY CAROL TERSINE (opposite): Bridge on Knight Road.

DELICATE BRANCH BY KATIE BALLANTINE (above): A snow covered branch in my yard.

PAGOPHOBIA 3 BY ETHAN QUIN (right): At a very slippery Whitehall area park.

SNOW BY LAURIE MCCARTY (left): An early spring?

THE COLD OF WINTER
BY OMAR MORALES (bottom left): Taken on Meuser Park, Wilson, Penn.

FROZEN
BY KERRY SNYDER (bottom right): Some of the awesome natural ice sculptures on the frozen shores of the Delaware River.

Help Find the Best of the Greater Lehigh Valley

Join the community of Greater Lehigh Valley photographers and enthusiasts!

Vote to find the best of the Greater Lehigh Valley, order prints or upload your own take on the Greater Lehigh Valley at:

capturelehighvalley.com

Community Stats

The Capture Greater Lehigh Valley book was created by the efforts of Greater Lehigh Valley folks who have a passion for their local community and an eye for great photography. The community of users at Capture Greater Lehigh Valley (capturelehighvalley.com) has spent countless hours shaping this book with submissions, votes and comments. Its their editing power that determined which photos deserved publication in this book and which photos our editors had to consider for publication. Along the way, users generated some astounding statistics (below) in terms of activity on the Capture Greater Lehigh Valley web site. Our sincere thanks to every user who dedicated their time to shaping the Capture Greater Lehigh Valley book.

15,297
photos

356
photographers

444,770
votes

21,473
comments

1,523
users

38,187
loves

Community Leaders

The active online community of users at Capture Greater Lehigh Valley (capturelehighvalley.com) shaped this book with its submissions, votes, comments, etc. Below you'll find the community leaders in each of six categories: top voter, the user with the most votes cast; top promoter, the user who promoted the contest via email the most; most followed, the user whom other users followed most; top commenter, the user who commented on photos the most; most decorated, the user with the most photo awards; and most dug, the user with the most "dig it" votes across all photos.

1. Top voter
Laurie McCarty
13,980 votes cast

2. Top promoter
Gene Fernandez
321 shares

3. Most followed
Gene Fernandez
95 followers

4. Top commenter
Tom Scherer
2,190 comments

5. Most decorated
Tim Holmes
54 photo awards

6. Most Dug
Tim Holmes
22,878 dig it votes

Winners

When picking from 15,297 photos, it's difficult to nail down what separates the best from the rest — especially when so many photos are so good. To help, we enlisted thousands of local folks to vote for their favorite shots. The response was epic: 444,770 votes were cast. The voting helped shape what would eventually be published in this book. Along the way, the votes produced the grand-prize and cover winners below.

Grand-prize winner
Farm in the Fall by Tom Scherer
Page 97

Cover winner
Stearman Love by Stacie McKeever
Cover, page 36

Runners-up
These photos finished just behind the grand-prize photo in total score.

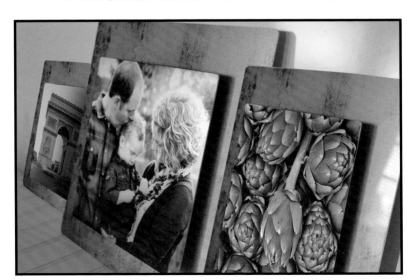

Many thanks to our sponsors!

THE BAUM SCHOOL OF ART

www.CardinalCamera.com

The mission of The Baum School of Art is to enrich lives through arts education. Our vision as a community art school is to be dedicated to providing instruction, guidance and encouragement for children and adults who wish to reach their full technical, physical, spiritual, creative and emotional potential through the study of the visual arts. Our work is deeply rooted in providing quality service to the community. Each year, nearly 2,500 students attend classes in drawing, painting, ceramics, sculpture, jewelry and metalsmithing, fashion design and construction, photography, graphic design, illustration, watercolor, and others. The school is accredited by the Accrediting Commission for Community and Pre-collegiate Arts Schools.

Currently Cardinal Camera has a 6000 sq. ft. location and is one of the largest volume camera stores in the United States. Cardinal Camera features the most modern on site processing of prints, enlargements, E-6, and digital products.

ArtsQuest's popular holiday marketplace! Recognized by Travel and Leisure Magazine as one of the top holiday markets in the world, Christkindlmarkt Bethlehem showcases aisles of exquisite handmade works by the nations finest artisans, the heart-warming sounds of live Christmas music, delicious food and more. Be sure to stop by the glassblowing booth, where beautiful ornaments and decorations are always being made. You can even try your hand at making your own glass ornament, perfect for gift giving or the family's Christmas Tree.

Since 1964, we have been building quality custom homes as well as constructing residential remodeling, additions, and commercial projects. Building a home is a big and very important decision and we have a dedicated and knowledgeable team to assist you through the entire building process. We have been recognized with many building awards including awards for our "universal designed" homes that incorporate numerous design features to allow for an "aging in place" home. All Curtis E. Schneck homes are designed and built to meet the owners individual needs and possess high quality workmanship and energy efficiency.

SmileKrafters is a multi-specialty dental center conveniently located near I-78 on Cedar Crest Boulevard in Allentown, across from the Lehigh Valley Hospital. Our team is a combination of general dentists, orthodontists, pedodontists, endodontists, periodontists & oral surgeons all under one roof!

Services at our state of the art facility include pediatric dentistry, braces, cosmetic dentistry, oral surgery, gum surgery, implants, and any other procedure you may need.

At SmileKrafters, we're all here for you! Call us at 610-628-1228 to schedule an appointment and get the smile you deserve.

TeleBear's Cub Club is for PBS39's youngest viewers (under age 10.) In addition to supporting the one-of-a-kind, educational programming not found anywhere else, members of the Club enjoy events, free passes to the region's premiere attractions (like Lehigh Valley Zoo), free meals at kid-friendly restaurants (like Applebee's), on-air birthday greetings, a newsletter and more. Right now, viewers are encouraged to enter TeleBear's Dance Contest! Simply post a short video of your child's best dance moves on TeleBear's Cub Club Facebook page and they could be on TV or win a fabulous prize, like tickets to Sesame Street Live!

lehighvalleylive.com

POWERED BY THE EXPRESS-TIMES

Lehighvalleylive.com provides consumers with information such as breaking news, multimedia, sports, jobs, autos, real estate, entertainment, weather, blogs and shopping, making it the #1 local online destination in the Lehigh Valley

QNB
Your Community Bank

Our vision: We will help you achieve your goals by providing a total financial relationship built upon exceptional personal service and a sincere interest in your success.